A Guide for Using

Old Yeller

in the Classroom

Based on the novel written Fred Gipson

*This guide written by **Michael H. Levin***
*and illustrated by **Cheryl Buhler***

Teacher Created Resources, Inc.
6421 Industry Way
Westminster, CA 92683
www.teachercreated.com
ISBN: 978-1-55734-427-4
©1993 Teacher Created Resources, Inc.
Reprinted, 2008
Made in U.S.A.

Table of Contents

Introduction

A good book can touch our lives like a good friend. Within its pages are words and characters that can inspire us to achieve our highest ideals. We can turn to it for companionship, recreation, comfort, and guidance. It can also give us a cherished story to hold in our hearts forever.

In *Literature Units,* great care has been taken to select books that are sure to become good friends!

Teachers who use this unit will find the following features to supplement their own valuable ideas.

- Sample Lesson Plans
- Pre-reading Activities
- A Biographical Sketch and Picture of the Author
- A Book Summary
- Vocabulary Lists and Suggested Vocabulary Activities
- Chapters grouped for study with each section including
    - *quizzes*
    - *hands-on projects*
    - *cooperative learning activities*
    - *cross-curriculum connections*
    - *extensions into the reader's own life*
- Post-reading Activities
- Book Report Ideas
- Research Ideas
- Culminating Activity
- Three Different Options for Unit Tests
- Bibliography
- Answer Key

We are confident this unit will be a valuable addition to your planning, and we hope your students will increase the circle of "friends" they have in books!

Sample Lesson Plan

Each of the lessons suggested below can take from one to several days to complete.

LESSON 1
- Introduce and complete some or all of the prereading activities found on page 5.
- Read "About the Author" with your students. (page 6)
- Introduce the vocabulary list for Section 1. (page 8)

LESSON 2
- Read Chapters 1 through 3. As you read, place the vocabulary words in the context of the story and discuss their meanings.
- Choose a vocabulary activity. (page 9)
- Make soap. (page 11)
- Discuss and write about being left in charge. (page 12)
- Study the book in terms of history and geography. (page 13)
- Begin Reading Response Journals. (page 14)
- Administer the Section 1 quiz. (page 10)
- Introduce the vocabulary list for Section 2. (page 8)

LESSON 3
- Read Chapters 4 through 6. Place the vocabulary words in context and discuss their meanings.
- Choose a vocabulary activity. (page 9)
- Learn about the movement and strength of the wind. (page 16)
- Create a Big Windy. (page 17)
- Discuss the book in terms of math. (page 18)
- Entertain your class. (page 19)
- Administer Section 2 quiz. (page 15)
- Introduce the vocabulary list for Section 3. (page 8)

LESSON 4
- Read Chapters 7 through 9. Place the vocabulary words in context and discuss their meanings.
- Choose a vocabulary activity. (page 9)
- Learn about and try growing corn. (page 21)
- Discuss onomatopoeia and find examples. (page 22)
- Create your own brand. (page 23)
- Explore different constellations. (page 24)
- Administer Section 3 quiz. (page 20)
- Introduce the vocabulary list for Section 4. (page 8)

LESSON 5
- Read Chapters 10 through 12. Place the vocabulary words in context and discuss their meanings.
- Choose a vocabulary activity. (page 9)
- Cook some regional dishes. (page 26)
- Discuss your pets. (page 27)
- Find out about canine diseases. (page 28)
- Rename familiar places. (page 29)
- Administer Section 4 quiz. (page 25)
- Introduce the vocabulary list for Section 5. (page 8)

LESSON 6
- Read Chapters 13 through 16. Place the vocabulary words in context and discuss their meanings.
- Choose a vocabulary activity. (page 9)
- Create a storyboard. (page 31)
- Discover foreshadowing. (page 32)
- Practice pantomime by doing some charades. (page 33)
- Discuss becoming an adult. (page 34)
- Administer Section 5 quiz. (page 30)

LESSON 7
- Discuss any questions your students have about the story. (page 35)
- Assign book reports and research activities. (pages 36 and 37)
- Begin work on culminating activities. (pages 38-41)

LESSON 8
- Administer Unit Tests: 1, 2, and/or 3. (pages 42, 43, and 44)
- Discuss the test answers and possibilities.
- Discuss the students' enjoyment of the book.
- Provide a list of related reading for your students. (page 45)

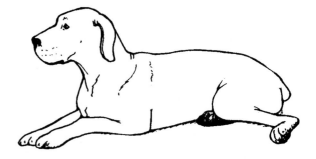

Before the Book

Before you begin reading *Old Yeller* with your students, do some pre-reading activities to stimulate interest and enhance comprehension. Here are some activities that might work for your class.

1. Predict what the story might be about just by hearing the title.

2. Predict what the story might be about just by looking at the cover illustration.

3. Discuss other books by Fred Gipson that students may have heard about or read.

4. Answer these questions:

   - Are you interested in:

     - stories about children and their pets?

     - stories about the old West?

     - stories with adventure and life or death struggles?

     - stories about dealing with young people having experiences that make them grow up?

     - stories that show a young person is capable of making important decisions and taking action?

     - stories that depict how life continues even after tragedy strikes?

   - Why might a person need to kill a dog?

   - How could a dog make someone angry?

   - In what ways can a dog be a useful pet?

   - Do you have a dog? What makes your dog special?

   - Should people be allowed to cry when they feel sad?

5. Work in groups to create a factual and/or fictional story about a dog.

6. Write descriptions or brainstorm ideas about what makes a person strong or courageous in the face of tragedy. Determine what the source of such strength might be.

7. Use the picture on page 48 to help introduce *Old Yeller* to your class. The picture can also be used as a journal cover for Reading Response Journals or as the centerpiece of a bulletin board display of student work.

About the Author

Fred Gipson was born February 7, 1908, in Mason, Texas, to Beckton and Emma (Dieshler) Gipson. He went to the University of Texas from 1933-1937. He married Tommie Eloise Wynn in 1930 and had two sons, Phillip Michael and Thomas Beckton.

He began writing in 1938 becoming a reporter for the *Corpus Christi Caller.* His first book was *Fabulous Empire* in 1946. *Old Yeller* was written in 1956 and remains Gipson's most famous novel. He won several awards for *Old Yeller* including a Newbery Honor Book award.

Fred Gipson wrote many other books about the West. These include *Hound-Dog Man* (1950), *The Trail Driving Rooster* (1955), *Cow Killers* (1956), and *Savage Sam* (1962).

Gipson went to Hollywood to write the screenplays for several of his novels. *Old Yeller* and *Savage Sam* were made into movies by Walt Disney Productions.

In his later life, Gipson raised cattle and hogs on his farm, and enjoyed hunting deer, wild turkey, quail and doves. He preferred fly fishing to all other sports. Gipson died in 1973 in the same town where he was born.

Many young people have learned much about the West from reading Fred Gipson's novels. He once said, "I've always liked true adventure tales and have always felt that I learned more history of my country from these tales than I ever did from the history books."

(Quotations and information from *Something About the Author,* edited by Anne Commire, Gale Research, Detroit, 1971)

Old Yeller

by Fred Gipson

(Harper Collins, 1956)

(Also available in Canada, UK, and Australia from Harper Collins)

Old Yeller takes place in the Hill Country of Texas in the late 1860's. It concerns the maturing of a young boy who must fight against his own worries as well as against the dangerous Texas frontier. The story can be considered on many levels, but it is first and foremost an exciting adventure of a boy and his dog.

Travis Coates takes over for his father who must drive cattle to market. Travis is fairly sure of himself as his father leaves the boy in charge of the family for several months. Young Travis is certain he can handle all situations and scoffs at his mother's suggestion that he needs a good dog. Travis has just lost his last dog and feels no animal could replace the one he had.

When Old Yeller appears it is Travis' younger brother, Arliss, who wants a dog. Travis fights against giving his love to this ugly, dingy yellow dog, but his mother immediately sees how this animal would fill an important need at the farm. After several occurrences, including saving Arliss from an angry bear, Old Yeller is accepted by the older boy.

Old Yeller becomes indispensible to the Coates family as he helps them in the many chores around the farm as well as saving Travis from being killed by wild pigs. Unfortunately, in protecting the mother and a neighbor girl from a mad wolf, the dog contracts hydrophobia. Travis must summon the courage to shoot his beloved companion when he realizes there is no way to save Old Yeller.

When the father returns to the family, he learns of all that Travis has done and tells the boy that "you couldn't ask more of a grown man." But Travis is too broken-hearted to hear the words he would have been proud to hear only a few days before. Yet when his father tells him that life is both good and bad and "a man can't afford to waste all the good part, worrying about the bad parts," Travis comes to terms with all that has happened.

Vocabulary Lists

On this page are vocabulary lists which correspond to each sectional grouping of chapters. Vocabulary activity ideas can be found on page 9 of this book.

SECTION 1
(Chapters 1-3)

aggravation	gnawed
brand	plunder
bray	solemn
clout	sulk
depredations	trifled
dingy	varmints
fierce	venison
frazzle	withers
gnarled	writhing (writhe)

SECTION 2
(Chapters 4-6)

astride	lunge
careened	marrow
clamoring	poultice
hauling	pounced
heave	riled
hydrophobia	shiftless
knoll	spasms
liable	sumptuous

SECTION 3
(Chapters 7-9)

baying	marveled
blizzard	panic
calve	plague
carcass	precious
castration	rouge
commotion	sighed
flinched	sober
heifer	thicket

SECTION 4
(Chapters 10-12)

anxious	pestering
coaxed	quiver
entrails	searing
fangs	squeamish
flustered	stunned
fringed	turpentine
gash	wretch

SECTION 5
(Chapters 13-16)

evidently	nettles
hideous	staggered
hulk	stench
buzzards	tote

8

Vocabulary Activity Ideas

You can help your students learn and retain the vocabulary in *Old Yeller* by providing them with interesting vocabulary activities. Here are some ideas to try.

❏ People of all ages like to make and solve puzzles. Ask your students to make their own **Crossword Puzzles** or **Wordsearch Puzzles** using the vocabulary words from the story.

❏ Challenge your students to a **Vocabulary Bee!** This is similar to a spelling bee, but in addition to spelling each word correctly, the game participants must correctly define the words as well.

❏ Play **Vocabulary Concentration.** The goal of this game is to match vocabulary words with their definitions. Divide the class into groups of 2-5 students. Have students make two sets of the cards the same size and color. On one set have them write the vocabulary words. On the second set have them write the definitions. All cards are mixed together and placed face down on a table. A player picks two cards. If the pair matches the word with its definitions, the player keeps the cards and takes another turn. If the cards don't match, they are returned to their places face down on the table, and another player takes a turn. Players must concentrate to remember the locations of the words and their definitions. The game continues until all matches have been made. This is an ideal activity for free exploration time.

❏ Have your students practice their writing skills by creating sentences and paragraphs in which multiple vocabulary words are used correctly. Ask them to share their **Compact Vocabulary** sentences and paragraphs with the class.

❏ Ask your students to create paragraphs which use the vocabulary words to present **History Lessons** that relate to the time period of the novel.

❏ Challenge your students to use a specific vocabulary word from the story at least **10 Times in One Day.** They must keep a record of when, how, and why the word was used.

❏ As a group activity, have students work together to create an **Illustrated Dictionary** of the vocabulary words.

❏ Play **20 Clues** with the entire class. In this game, one student selects a vocabulary word and gives clues about this word, one by one, until someone in the class can guess the word.

❏ Play **Vocabulary Charades.** In this game, vocabulary words are acted out!

You probably have many more ideas to add to this list. Try them! See if experiencing vocabulary on a personal level increases your students' vocabulary interest and retention.

What Do You Know?

Answer the following questions about Chapters 1, 2, and 3.

1. What are two reasons the Coates family called the dog Old Yeller?

   _____

   _____

2. In what state does the family live and in approximately what year?

   _____

   _____

3. Why does the Father (Papa) need to leave his family?

   _____

   _____

4. When Papa leaves, what responsibilities fall to Travis?

   _____

   _____

5. How does Travis prove from the beginning that he can handle things in Papa's absence?

   _____

   _____

6. What does Travis want Papa to bring him?

   _____

   _____

7. What are two instances that make Travis angry at Old Yeller?

   _____

   _____

8. Why does Travis need to kill a doe?

   _____

   _____

9. What does Travis think will convince Mama to get rid of Old Yeller?

   _____

   _____

10. Describe the relationship between Travis and his little brother, Arliss.

    _____

    _____

Making Soap

In the area of Texas where Travis lived with his Mama, Papa, and little brother, there were no cities. In fact, towns were scarce. Most people lived in isolated areas where neighbors were often miles away. Since there were no stores, the settlers had to make just about everything they used.

One product that had to be made was soap. This item we use every day and can buy at any store was not taken for granted in frontier days. It was more difficult to keep clean then without modern conveniences like indoor plumbing, washing machines, and vacuum cleaners. Soap was a very important commodity!

Pioneers usually made soap from grease and wood ashes, but a batch can be made with salad oil and baking soda.

Materials

¼ cup (60 mL) each of salad oil, baking soda, and water; glass pan; wooden spoon; glass jar with lid; hot plate

Preparation

Since heating is involved, the teacher might want to demonstrate for the class, using students as assistants.

Directions

1. Combine salad oil, baking soda, and water in a glass pan.

2. Simmer over low heat. Stir with a wooden or plastic spoon. (Do not use a metal one.)

3. After mixture thickens, heat for a few more minutes.

4. Remove from burner to cool. The mixture will separate with the oil on the top and a white mixture on the bottom.

5. In a glass jar pour one teaspoon (5 mL) of the soap and two cups (500 mL) of hot water.

6. Screw on the lid before shaking.

As you shake the jar, watch the soap suds appear!

Because the combining and processing is often hit-or-miss, you probably should not wash with the soap. But it will clean out any drain you pour it down!

Left in Charge

When Travis' father leaves for the cattle drive, Travis is put in charge of many of the farm jobs and the family security. In Chapter 1, he says to Travis:

> *"Now Travis, you 're getting to be a big boy; and while I'm gone, you'll be the man of the family. I want you to act like one. You take care of Mama and Little Arliss. You Look after the work and don't wait around for your mama to point out what needs to be done. Think you can do that?"*

In a group, discuss the following questions. Choose one person to record the answers on the lines. When you are finished, compare and contrast your responses with those of other groups.

- If your mother or father left you in charge of the work around the house, what extra jobs would you have to do?

_____

- Would you be able to handle these responsibilities? All of them? Some of them? Explain.

_____

- What does Travis' father mean when he says he expects Travis to act like a man? Do most fourteen year olds act grown-up? Explain, using examples from your experience.

_____

Travis' father continues:

> *"You act a man's part while I'm gone, and I'll see that you get a man's horse to ride when I sell the cattle. I think we can shake on that deal. "*

- How is Travis' father treating him like a grown-up?

_____

- The father makes a bargain or agreement with his son. Explain what an agreement is.

_____

- Is it fair for the father to make a bargain like this with his son? Explain your feelings.

_____

- Do your parents make bargains or agreements with you? What kind? How do the agreements work out?

_____

Texas Facts

Directions: Use appropriate reference books to locate the following information about the state of Texas.

Population: _____(ranks_____ in population)

Area: _____square miles (ranks_____in size)

Capital: _____

Capital City Population: _____

State Nickname: _____

State Flower: _____

State Motto: _____

Highest Point in Texas: _____

Lowest Point in Texas: _____

Time Zones:_____

Three Largest Cities and Their Populations:

1._____   _____

2._____   _____

3._____   _____

Find the city of Mason on a map of Texas. This small town is the county seat of Mason County in the Hill Country of Central Texas.

- What larger town is approximately 40 miles south of Mason?_____

- What U.S. Army fort is approximately 100 miles northeast of Mason?_____

- What lake and dam is approximately 50 miles east of Mason? _____

- What river runs a few miles south of Mason?_____

- What town (with a Spanish name and famous underground caverns) is approximately 80 miles west of Mason?

  _____

- The largest city in Texas is approximately 120 miles southeast of Mason. What is it? _____

  _____

Reading Response Journals

One great way to insure that the reading of *Old Yeller* becomes a personal experience for each student is to include the use of Reading Response Journals in your plans. In these journals, students can be encouraged to respond to the story in a number of ways. Here are a few ideas.

- Tell students that the purpose of the journal is to record their thoughts, ideas, observations, and questions as they read *Old Yeller.*
- Provide students with, or ask them to suggest, topics from the story that would stimulate writing. Here are a few examples from the chapters in Section 1:
  - Farm life is different from living in the city, whether over 100 years ago or now. What is special about living on a farm?

  - Was it fair for the father to leave Travis with so much responsibility? Was he asking too much of a fourteen year old?

  - Travis feels that because he is fourteen years old, he should not cry when his father leaves. Is it permissible for a boy to cry when he feels like it?

- After the reading of each chapter, students can write one or more new things they learned in the chapter.
- Ask students to draw their responses to certain events or characters in the story, using the blank pages in their journals.
- Tell students that they may use their journals to record "diary-type" responses that they may want to enter.
- Encourage students to bring their journal ideas to life! Ideas generated from their journal writing can be used to create plays, debates, stories, songs, and art displays.
- Give students quotes from the novel and ask them to write their own responses. Make sure to do this before you go over the quotations in class. In groups they could list the different ways students can respond to the same quote.

Allow students time to write in their journals daily. Explain to the students that their Reading Response Journals can be evaluated in a number of ways. Here are a few ideas.

- Personal reflections will be read by the teacher, but no corrections or letter grades will be assigned. Credit is given for effort, and all students who sincerely try will be awarded credit. If a grade is desired for this type of entry, grade according to the number of journal entries completed. For example, if five journal assignments were made and the student conscientiously completes all five, then he or she receives an "A."

- Nonjudgemental teacher responses should be made as you read journals to let the students know you are reading and enjoying their journals. Here are some types of responses that will please your journal writers and encourage them to write more.
  — "You have really found what's important in the story!"
  — "You write so clearly, I almost feel as if I am there."
  — "If you feel comfortable, I'd like for you to share this with the class. I think they'll enjoy it as much as I have."

What Do You Know?

Answer the following questions about Chapters 4, 5, and 6.

1. On the back of this paper, write a one paragraph summary of the major events that happened in these three chapters. Then complete the rest of the questions on this page.

2. Why does Old Yeller run away during the bull fight after Travis tells him to go after the bulls?

_____

_____

3. What happens that makes Travis say that the Chongo (Mexican for 'droop horn') "was suddenly the silliest looking bull you ever saw."

_____

_____

4. How does the fight of the bulls teach Travis that he must think ahead?

_____

_____

5. According to Travis, what does Little Arliss do with "every living thing that ran, flew, jumped, or crawled"?

_____

_____

6. How is Old Yeller able to save Little Arliss when his brother and mother were not able to?

_____

_____

7. The reader sees how smart Old Yeller is during this incident with the bear. The dog knows that the bear is too big and strong for him. How is Old Yeller able to keep the bear away from the family?

_____

_____

8. How does Travis feel about Old Yeller after the bear fight? Why?

_____

_____

9. Who are Bud Searcy and Lisbeth?

_____

_____

10. What does Lisbeth promise Travis she will not tell? Why does she promise this?

_____

_____

Which Way the Wind?

In Chapter 3, Travis is able to tell the direction of the wind by licking one finger and holding it up and feeling which side is coolest. There are many ways of seeing which way the wind is blowing. Some are very simple, while others (used by meteorologists) are complicated and expensive.

These simple projects can tell us the direction from which the wind is blowing and how hard it blows. Follow these simple instructions.

Paper Wind Sock

Materials: one full, folded sheet of newspaper (no color print) per student; tape; string; wire; glue; crayons or pastels; scissors; stick or dowel

Directions:

* Draw a fish profile on the folded sheet of newspaper, making sure the back (top) of the fish is on the folded edge. Cut out the fish shape; do not cut the fold.
* Open the fish and lay it flat. Add additional fins, if desired. Use crayons or pastels to decorate the fish, making each side the same.
* Fold and glue the top and bottom edges of the fish closed. Do not glue mouth. Stuff loosely with newspaper wads through the tail opening. Glue the tail closed.
* To strengthen the mouth, tape a piece of wire (wire will allow you to shape the mouth) along the inside mouth edge; then fold the edge of the paper over the wire mouth twice and glue down. Shape the mouth. Tape the ends of three 6" (15 cm) pieces of string to the mouth opening. Tie the other ends together. Tie one end of a longer piece of string to the 6" strings. Attach the long string to a stick or dowel which will be used to hold the wind sock.
* Take your wind socks outside and try them. Find out which way wind is blowing.

Making An Anemometer

An anemometer is a wind gauge that tells how hard the wind is blowing.

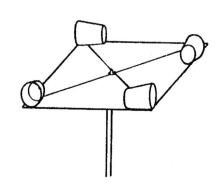

Materials: For each group of 3 or 4 students you will need: 4 paper cups; 12" (30 cm) square piece of cardboard; 18" (46 cm) dowel; long straight pin; pencil; bead; ruler; tape or glue

Directions:

* Using a ruler, draw a diagonal line across the cardboard, corner to corner. Draw another diagonal line across joining the other two corners.
* Place cups on their sides and glue one to each corner of the cardboard. Be sure cup openings face the same direction (see diagram).
* Push the straight pin down though the center of the cardboard, where the lines cross.
* Put the pin through the bead. Gently tap the pin into the tip of the dowel.
* Take your wind gauge outside and "find" some wind.

A Big Windy

In Chapter 5, Arliss tells a tale "about how he'd dived 'way down into a deep hole under the rocks and dragged that fish out and nearly got drowned before he could swim to the bank with it."

Travis calls the tale a "big windy." There are other names for telling a story such as that: a tall tale, a big whopper, a "fish story." In American literature, tall tales are well known. They usually start with real people. Then as stories are told and retold, they become more and more exaggerated. Some real people that have had tall tales told about them are Paul Bunyan (and Babe, his Blue Ox), Calamity Jane, John Henry, and Pecos Bill. Pecos Bill stories are especially interesting since they take place in an area not too far from the location of *Old Yeller.*

In a group, try to invent a tall tale. Your group will need four or five members. Number off. The first person will begin. Orally, with each member spinning his part of the yarn for two minutes, try and make your section full of exaggeration. After the last person is done, write your version of what you heard. You can add any new ideas you had while listening or writing.

Here are some suggestions for starting:

- Once there was a girl who found a baby mountain lion...
- The Smith Clan of Ashtabula, Ohio, were the most famous circus family in history...
- Big Bob was the strongest man ever seen in the state of Texas...
- Ms. Sandra Kaputnik was the hardest 6th grade teacher the city of Kalamazoo, Michigan, had ever known...
- Trina and Trisha were twin sisters who had a large collection of animals at their small house...

Figuring the Mileage

Old Yeller takes place in the central Texas area called the Hill Country. This is marked on the map below by the town of Mason. Study this map. Notice how far the cities are from one another. Figure the mileage in miles or kilometers (1 mile = 1.609 km) between the cities named in the questions below.

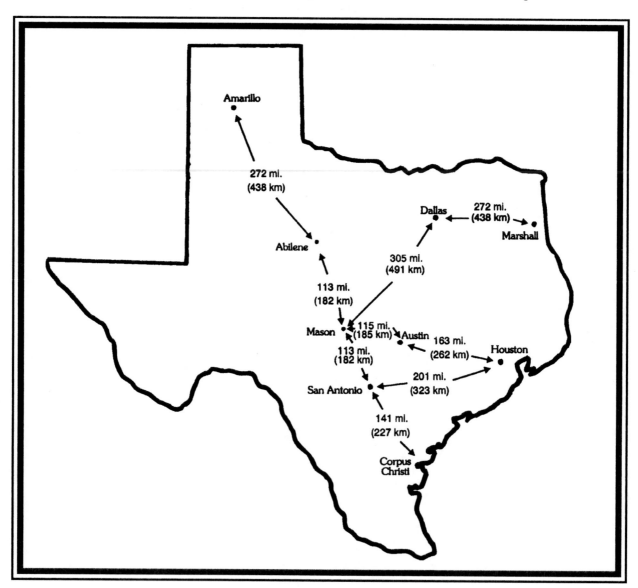

1. How many miles/kilometers is it from Mason to Marshall by way of Dallas? _____

2. If you travel by way of Austin, how many miles/kilometers is it from Mason to Houston? _____

3. Is it closer to go from Mason to Houston by way of San Antonio or Austin? _____

4. Taking the most southerly route, how far is it from Abilene to Corpus Christi? _____

5. Is it closer to Amarillo or Marshall from Mason?_____

6. Make up 5 mileage questions of your own using the map on this page. Be sure to include an answer key. Ask a classmate to answer the questions.

That's Entertainment!

In Chapter 4 of *Old Yeller,* Travis, Little Arliss and their mother get a surprise opportunity for some exciting entertainment as two bulls decide to have a fight near their cabin. The family sits on the fence rails, viewing the battle as if they were watching a show. What do you like to do for entertainment? Think about the following questions. Discuss your ideas and opinions with classmates. Then try the activity at the bottom of the page.

- What is your definition of entertainment?
- What kind of television program do you like the best? Why?
- Have you seen a movie lately that you really enjoyed? What was it and what made it special?
- Do you listen to music on the radio or have a tape or CD player? What is your favorite kind of music?
- Have you been to a sports event in the past year? What was it? What did you enjoy most about it?
- Have you ever seen a live performance (besides a sporting event)? What was it and what did you like about it?

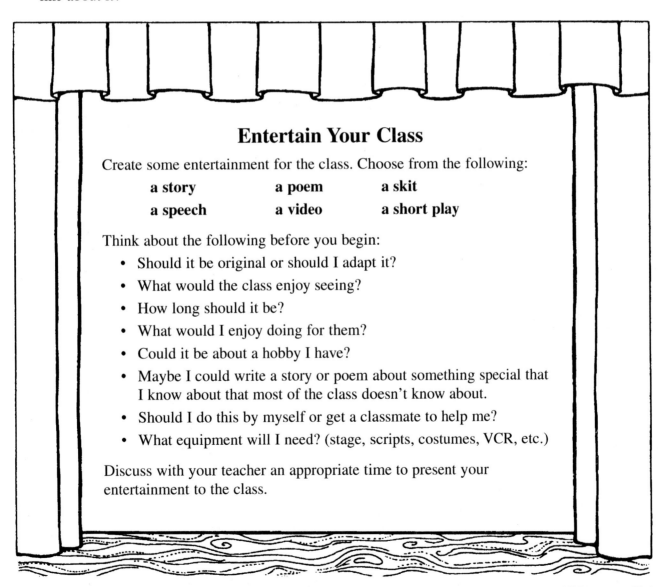

Entertain Your Class

Create some entertainment for the class. Choose from the following:

a story	**a poem**	**a skit**
a speech	**a video**	**a short play**

Think about the following before you begin:
- Should it be original or should I adapt it?
- What would the class enjoy seeing?
- How long should it be?
- What would I enjoy doing for them?
- Could it be about a hobby I have?
- Maybe I could write a story or poem about something special that I know about that most of the class doesn't know about.
- Should I do this by myself or get a classmate to help me?
- What equipment will I need? (stage, scripts, costumes, VCR, etc.)

Discuss with your teacher an appropriate time to present your entertainment to the class.

What Do You Know?

Answer the following questions about Chapters 7, 8, and 9.

1. On the back of this paper, write a one paragraph summary of the major events that happened in these three chapters. Then complete the rest of the questions on this page.

2. Why does Old Yeller begin sleeping in the boys' bedroom?

   _____

   _____

3. Why do Travis and Old Yeller spend some nights in the corn patch?

   _____

   _____

4. How does Spot get tamed and turned into a good milk cow?

   _____

   _____

5. When Burn Sanderson comes to the farm, what is he looking for?

   _____

   _____

6. Why doesn't Sanderson take Old Yeller with him?

   _____

   _____

7. What deadly disease does Sanderson warn Travis about?

   _____

   _____

8. Since the hogs are allowed to roam free like range cattle, how can the settlers tell who the hogs belong to?

   _____

   _____

9. What is Travis' system for rounding up the pigs?

   _____

   _____

10. How does Old Yeller help in rounding up the pigs?

   _____

   _____

Growing Corn

In Chapter 7, Travis and Old Yeller keep watch over the corn crop. Corn was an important crop for the Coates family both as food for them and for the animals. Without a good crop, they might not be able to get through the year.

Corn, also called maize, was first found in North America. The Native Americans began collecting it and using it for food almost 10,000 years ago. From that time on, the use of corn has increased so much that it is now one of the world's most important crops.

For this activity you are going to plant and grow your own corn.

Materials: 2 or 3 corn seeds per student; clear plastic cups; soil; water

Directions: Fill a clear, plastic cup with soil halfway to the top. Plant 2 or 3 corn seeds near the sides of the cup and cover with soil. Water the seeds, until the soil is moist (like a wrung out washcloth). Continue to keep moist, but not soggy. Provide full sunlight. When the plants reach 6" (15 cm) tall, they may be transplanted to the ground.

In the boxes below, draw what your plant looks like as it grows.

Week 1	**Week 2**
Week 3	**Week 4**

What did you learn? _____

_____

_____

Onomatopoeia

Onomatopoeia is the use of words to imitate sounds. Young children use this kind of language when they call a dog a "bow-wow," or a train a "choo-choo." "Bow-wow" sounds like a dog barking, and "choo-choo" resembles the sound of a puffing locomotive. Other onomatopoeic words are snap, crunch, fizz, and hush. Writers use onomatopoeia because it can give a double emphasis to their work. A reader gets meaning from the printed word and receives additional meaning from the sound of that word.

In *Old Yeller,* author Fred Gipson often uses onomatopoeic words to help the reader hear more clearly what he is trying to convey to them. The special words add emphasis to the sentences. Look at the following sentences in which the onomatopoeic words are bolded.

> *"All he'd do was hang with that hind leg and let out one shrill **shriek** after another as fast as he could suck in a breath."* (How would the sentence be different if Gipson had used the word 'sound' instead?)

> *"The bulls **crashed** into the cabin again."* (Substitute 'ran' in the sentence. Which way makes the reader most aware of how the bulls hit the building? Why?)

Underline the onomatopoeic word(s) in each of the following sentences from the novel.

1. *"They grunted and strained and roared."*

2. *"Their horns and hoofs clattered against the logs."*

3. *"Why couldn't he keep his blabber mouth shut?"*

4. *"There went the frightened, snorting cattle, stampeding through the trees with their tails in the air like it was heel-fly time."*

5. *"Then he lifted his voice in a wild brassy blare that sent echoes clamoring in the draws and canyons for miles around."*

Discuss these special words in your group and with your teacher.

Work in groups to find and use more onomatopoeic words.

To help you get started, think about words we use to describe someone eating. How about words that describe a baseball hitting a mitt or a basketball bouncing against a backboard? Think of other soundalike words we use for animal noises.

Your group can probably come up with at least a dozen words that are onomatopoeic. Discuss how to put each one in an interesting sentence and have one group member record them. Share your sentences with the class.

As a class, choose several onomatopoeic words to display around the room. Each group could "sketch" the word letters in a way that expresses the meaning and sound. (See the example on this page.)

Branding

Travis must brand the hogs so that the different settlers can distinguish them. It was a dangerous job for Travis but his father had worked out a method and Old Yeller was there to help. In this activity you can create your own brand using a potato. Sound impossible? Not at all! And you will find it is fun.

Materials: ½ raw potato per student; paring knife; tempera paints; foam tray; large drawing paper or butcher paper; markers, pencils, or pens

Directions:

1. Cut potato in half.

2. Draw the pattern you have chosen on the surface of the cut side of the potato. Keep the design simple.

3. With a knife, cut an outline of your shape on the potato about ¼" (.6 cm) deep. Use the knife to chip away all the other parts around the shape. Do not cut into the design. The design should protrude about ¼" above the surface of the potato.

4. Dip the potato in the paint and stamp the print on your paper. Make interesting designs using your branding potato.

Constellations

Travis and Old Yeller must spend some nights in the corn fields fighting the boar coons. The nights are clear so the stars can be seen easily. Travis wonders what the stars are and "if Papa, 'way off up yonder in Kansas, could see the same stars I could see." Do you ever wonder if you are seeing the same stars where you live that people all over the world are seeing? What do you know about the stars? Look at the drawings and information about some of the many constellations (or star clusters) below. Try to find them in the night sky. Perhaps you can find some interesting facts about the 89 constellations in our sky.

Little Dipper—The first star in the handle of the Little Dipper is the North Star. The star always points north. The Little Dipper can be seen in the northern sky all year long.

Big Dipper—Use the Big Dipper to help find the North Star. Imagine a line running through the two outside stars of the cup. Keep looking up until the North Star is visible. Columbus and other sailors knew that the North Star held its position in the sky while all the other star groups kept moving.

Draco—According to Greek legend, Ladon, the sleeping dragon, was told to guard Hera's apple tree. One day Heracles tricked Ladon and sliced off his head. To punish Ladon, Hera changed him into a constellation of stars.

Casseopeia—Casseopeia was a boastful queen who often bragged about her own and her daughter's beauty. The gods punished her by making her appear upside down. Thus, depending on the season, Casseopeia looks like a W or an M.

On Your Own Projects

- The Ancient Greeks used mythology to explain the various constellations. Research and write a report about how one of the constellations got its name. An excellent resource book for this project is *The Stargazer's Guide to the Galaxy* by Q.L. Pearce (RGA Publishing Group, 1991).
- In our sky there are 89 constellations. Find out some of them.
- Find out your astrological sign. Draw a picture of your sign's constellation.
- Read and learn the definition of "star."

What Do You Know?

Answer the following questions about Chapters 10, 11, and 12.

1. On the back of this paper, write a one paragraph summary of the major events that happened in these three chapters. Then complete the rest of the questions on this page.

2. Travis had never been to the far side of Salt Branch. Why is he excited about going there?

   _____

   _____

3. Instead of being in a tree above the hogs, what is Travis standing on this time? Why is this a mistake?

   _____

   _____

4. Where does Travis get slashed? How bad an injury is it?

   _____

   _____

5. After Travis' is cut, why doesn't he go directly home?

   _____

   _____

6. How does Travis react when his mother tells him to go to bed and not to walk on the leg for a week?

   _____

   _____

7. Why does Mama send Little Arliss off to look for a green-striped lizard?

   _____

   _____

8. How does the family manage to get Old Yeller home from Salt Branch?

   _____

   _____

9. Why does Mama have to do all the work herself now?

   _____

   _____

10. What does Lisbeth bring Travis as a present? How does Travis react?

    _____

    _____

Texas Recipes

Old Yeller takes place in the Hill Country of Texas. This is the area around Mason where the author was born. It is an area mainly settled by immigrants from Germany. Below are two regional recipes from this area your class might enjoy making. It seems fairly certain that they would have been favorites of Travis and other children in this area.

Potato Cakes (serves 6)

Ingredients:

2 cups (500 mL) raw grated potatoes (about 4 large)

2 eggs, separated

⅛ teaspoons (.6 mL) baking powder

1 teaspoon (5 mL) salt

1 tablespoon (15 mL) flour

¼ cup (60 mL) shortening

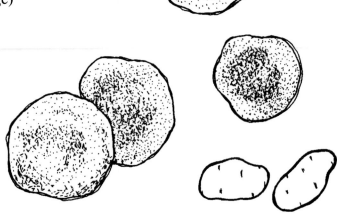

Directions:

Peel potatoes and soak in cold water for several hours. Grate and then drain well. It is important that all starch is removed. Beat egg yolks, stir into potatoes. Mix baking powder, salt, and flour together and stir into potato-egg mixture. Beat egg whites until stiff and fold into potatoes. Heat shortening in heavy skillet until very hot. (Make sure there is adult supervision at this point, or have an adult do this part with the students watching.) Drop potato mixture by spoonfuls in the hot shortening and fry until golden brown. Turn and brown on other side.

Peach Basket

Ingredients:

6 large cooked or canned peach halves
lettuce
¼ cup (60 mL) finely diced celery
¼ cup (60 mL) finely diced apple
⅛ cup (30 mL) mayonnaise
6 maraschino cherries

Directions:

Drain peaches. Place half of a peach on a piece of crisp lettuce. Fill with celery and apple mixture which has been moistened with mayonnaise. Garnish with cherries.

For Pets' Sake

Like most children who live on farms, Travis and Arliss are used to having animals around. Often, all the animals are expected to "earn their keep" or have specific jobs to do around the farm. In most families today, animals are kept only as pets. A pet is defined as an animal kept for pleasure or companionship. If there is a pet in the home, it is usually a dog or cat. However, there are many unusual pets that people keep in their homes. In a group of three or four, discuss the questions below about pets. Have one member of the group record the answers.

- What pets do members of your group own?

- Make a list of the different kinds of pets people you know have.

- What kinds of concerns must you consider before you acquire a pet?

- What animal makes the best pet? Have a debate in your group.

- What are the problems involved with having a pet? What pet causes the least problems? What pet causes the most problems?

- What sort of pet would be best for a young child to take care of? Why?

- In what situations would it be unfair to an animal to keep it as a pet?

- Are there any jobs a pet could do around a house? Explain.

Owning a pet requires commitment and responsibility. As a group, brainstorm a list of general guidelines which a person should follow in order to take proper care of his or her pet. Display the guidelines in a chart and present them to the class.

Canine Diseases and Parasites

Old Yeller was bitten by a wolf that had hydrophobia, or rabies. This caused the disease to go into Old Yeller's system. This meant that the dog would soon be having the same symptoms as the wolf, the bull, and the heifer, Spot.

Using appropriate reference materials, answer the following questions about hydrophobia on a separate piece of paper. Then, fill in the chart about other diseases that can infect dogs.

- What other animals, besides those mentioned in the novel, can spread hydrophobia?

- What are some of the symptoms of the disease in dogs?

- What are some of the symptoms of the disease in humans?

- How can humans be treated if they are bitten by a rabid animal?

- Who discovered a cure for rabies (when a human is bitten by a rabid animal)?

- In what year and country did this scientist discover the cure?

Disease or Parasite	Symptom(s)	Cure(s)
fleas		
ticks		
worms		
distemper		
canine hepatitis		
leptospirosis		

What's In a Name?

In *Old Yeller*, there are places Travis talks about that are named because of what the place looks like or what can be found near it. Salt Licks is the area near the Coates' house where the animals come to lick the salt in the rocks. Birdsong Creek was probably named for the birds that can be heard singing in the area.

Naming places in this way is a common practice. There are many famous places in the United States that have been named because of their geographic characteristics. Decide why the following areas are so named. Don't try to find the information in a book; use your imagination! When you are done, find the places in appropriate reference books and discover why they were given the names.

1. Yellowstone National Park (Wyoming)

2. Pebble Beach Golf Course (California)

3. Hot Springs (Arkansas)

4. Sweetwater (Texas)

5. Palm Beach (Florida)

Are there any places in your town or city that are named for what is around them? (Elm Street? Riverside Park? Hilltop School?) Write several examples and explain how you think each place got its name.

_____

_____

_____

_____

_____

Now let's do some re-naming. Forget those boring, meaningless names! Make up a new name for your school, the street you live on, the area your house is in, wherever! Re-name at least five places near your home. Make sure your new name matches a geographical landmark or other unique feature. Explain the reason you re-named each example. Have fun!

_____

_____

_____

_____

_____

What Do You Know?

Answer the following questions about Chapters 13, 14, 15, and 16.

1. On the back of this paper, write a two paragraph summary of the major events that happened in these three chapters. Then complete the rest of the questions on this page.

2. Although Travis doesn't think Lisbeth Searcy would be much help, she is. How does Lisbeth help the family?

_____

_____

3. What do Travis and Mama think is wrong with Spot at first?

_____

_____

4. Why does Mama say they have to burn the bull's carcass?

_____

_____

5. For the first time, Travis wishes that his father would come back quickly. What does Travis think he cannot handle?

_____

_____

6. How does Travis feel when Mama convinces him that Old Yeller will have to be shot? (Find a quote from the novel for your answer).

_____

_____

7. Does Travis hesitate in shooting Old Yeller? Why does Travis understand that the dog has to be killed?

_____

_____

8. Why isn't Travis excited about the horse his father brought for him?

_____

_____

9. What advice does Papa have for dealing with the kind of hurt Travis has?

_____

_____

10. What finally begins to make Travis feel that he is alive again?

_____

_____

Storyboard

A storyboard is similar to a comic strip. Look at the six blank areas in the storyboard below. Choose six main events that occurred in the chapters you have read in this section. Then, illustrate them in sequential order as they happened in the chapters. Finally, write a sentence describing the scene. Perhaps you will want to work in groups with one person drawing and another writing the captions.

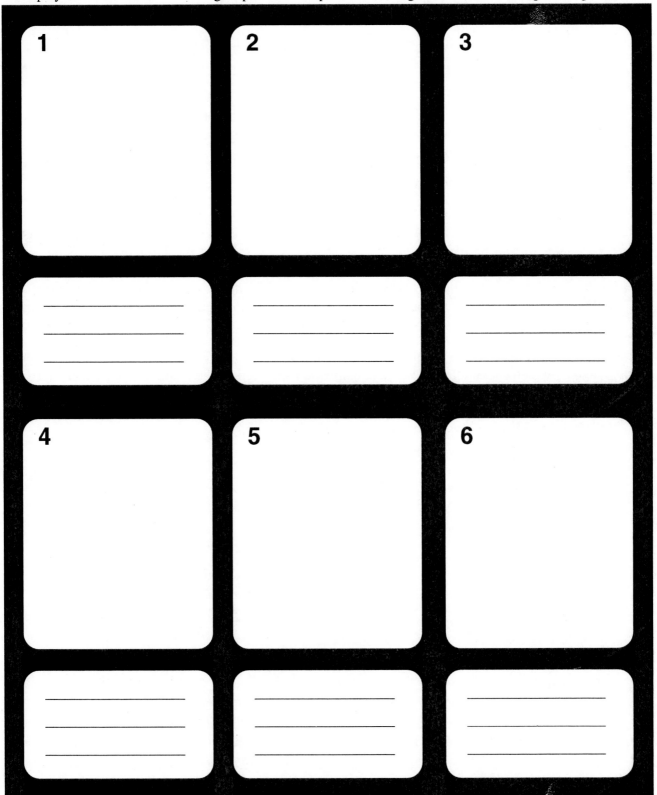

Foreshadowing

Foreshadowing is a technique authors use to give the reader, listener, or viewer of a story, movie, or play hints of what is to come. Foreshadowing serves two purposes: (1) It stimulates interest on the part of the reader to learn what happens next, and (2) it prepares the reader for the direction the plot will take, making it seem more real.

In *Old Yeller*, Fred Gipson uses foreshadowing a number of times to help Travis tell his story. This helps give the story a strong structure, and helps the reader to become more involved in what is going on. Here are some examples:

1. The first few paragraphs of the novel tell the reader how much Travis cared for Old Yeller and that he had to shoot him. *"He made me so mad at first that I wanted to kill him. Then later, when I had to kill him, it was like having to shoot some of my own folks."*

   So in a sense, the reader knows what will eventually happen to the dog, not why Travis had to kill his pet or why this was so difficult for him to do.

2. Look at this foreshadowing from Chapter 6: *"...when we remembered back, we realized that he hadn't eaten anything we'd fed him for the last several days. Yet he was fat with hair as slick and shiny as a dog eating three square meals a day."* This foreshadows the section later in the chapter when Lisbeth tells Travis that his "big yeller dog" was robbing the other farmers of the settlement of their eggs and meat. Even though Yeller did not eat anything at home, he was getting plenty to eat elsewhere.

In a group, discuss the following examples of foreshadowing. Then have one member write how your group members would explain the way each example helps to prepare the reader for what will happen.

- *"We located the hogs in plenty of time; but before we were done with them, I didn't want to go see a bat cave or anything else."* (Chapter 10)

- *"We could see the buzzards gathering long before we got there. We could see them wheeling black against the blue sky and dropping lower and lower with each circling...But when we moved down into the prickly-pearflats, my misery erased some. For suddenly, up out of a wash ahead rose a flurry of flapping wings. Something had disturbed those buzzards and I thought I knew what it was."* (Chapter 11)

- *" 'That pesky Spot, ' I heard (Mama) say impatiently. 'I don 't know what's got into her staying out all night like that and letting her calf go hungry.' "* (Chapter 13)

- *"At the last minute, Yeller got up off his cowhide. He stood watching (Mama and Lisbeth) a minute like he was trying to make up his mind about something; then he went trotting after them...I didn't call him back..it's a good thing I didn't."* (Chapter 14)

- *" 'Yessum, 'I said, 'It's sure a good thing that Old Yeller was along to keep him fought off ' Mama waited a little bit, then said in a quiet voice: 'It was a good thing for us, Son; but it wasn't good for Old Yeller.' "* (Chapter 15)

Mime Time

Although Travis did not have any time for games while his father was away, he probably enjoyed playing as much as any boy or girl. One game that was popular during the 1860's was charades. The game is still popular today and your class might enjoy trying some charades.

The basic idea is for someone to act out in pantomime a word (or a series or words) which an audience tries to guess. In a class, the game can be played with groups of 6-8 players. If your class is large, you can divide into four or five teams and have the winning team of each round play another winning group. One at a time the players of a given team act out their words while the other members of the team try to guess the charade. Each team performs the charade in the same way and is timed. After every team has had a turn, a timekeeper announces the team who finishes in the shortest amount of time as the winner. You can choose a non-player as the timekeeper or be the clock watcher yourself. Each person has up to two minutes to act out his/her charade. Remind students that it doesn't matter how the charades are solved as long as the "mime" does not make any noise.

Example:

Suppose that the charade is the phrase "as flat as a pancake." Since this phrase contains five words, the student would first show five fingers to teammates (indicating five words). When the team understands this, she then holds up one finger to indicate that she will now act out the first word of her charade. One signal that is used is for the student to hold a thumb and forefinger in the air about an inch apart, indicating a small word such as "and", "the", "or", or "as". The second word "flat" can be acted out by putting the hands together horizontally or by placing the hand cupping the ear to show that it is a rhyming word to the one acted out. Then the actor can "show" a hat or cat. The last word can be shown by "flipping pancakes."

Suggestions:

- Choose easy words at first so the students get the idea of the game. Colors, animals, vegetables, fruits, synonyms (quick and fast, look and see, late and tardy), and antonyms (bright and dull, plain and fancy, hit and miss) are good examples.

- You can have the charades already written down on pieces of paper which the students draw out of a hat, or allow them to write some for the other team.

- As they become used to the signals, you can try current movie titles, literature titles you have studied during the year, idioms, geographical names, or famous people in history.

Try it with your class. It can get noisy, but it will be fun!

Becoming an Adult

A common theme running through literature for young people is the passage from childhood to adulthood. Usually it deals with the child taking on certain responsibilities that show him or her acting more like an adult. In *Old Yeller*, Travis is given certain tasks to do by his father. As Travis performs these tasks, he understands that he must leave behind some of his childish ways of thinking in order to be responsible to his family.

1. The most difficult decision Travis has to make during the novel is to kill Old Yeller. His mother offers to do it for him. However, Travis says he will do it. Why does Travis decide to kill the dog himself? How does this show that Travis is becoming an adult?

_____

_____

_____

_____

2. What is the hardest decision you have had to make? How did you handle it? If you had to do it again, would you do it differently?

_____

_____

_____

_____

3. What do you think a young person needs to do in order to prove he or she is an adult? Do you think Travis proved he was an adult? Explain.

_____

_____

_____

_____

4. Describe an older teenager you know. Using the idea of taking responsibility, do you think that he or she acts more like an adult or a child? Explain your answer.

_____

_____

_____

Any Questions?

When you finished reading *Old Yeller*, did you have some questions that were left unanswered? Write them here.

_____

_____

_____

Then work in groups or by yourself to prepare possible answers for the questions you have asked above or those written below. When you have finished, share your ideas with the class.

- Does Travis go to school?
- What is the school like that Travis would go to?
- How did Old Yeller get his ear "chewed off"?
- How did Old Yeller learn all the things he knows?
- Why was Burn Sanderson so kind to allow the family to keep Old Yeller?
- Were there other families in the area around Salt Lick?
- How might a family get along without a father if they only had younger children like Little Arliss?
- What would have happened to Travis if Old Yeller hadn't been there to save him from the wild hogs?
- What would have happened to Mama and Lisbeth if Old Yeller hadn't gone with them to burn Spot's body?
- How would the story have been different if Papa had come back before Spot had gotten hydrophobia?
- How did Travis and the new pup that Lisbeth gave him get along?
- Did Travis and Lisbeth become good friends?
- How did Travis' life change after his father came home?
- Do you think it was necessary for the author to have Old Yeller killed? Why?
- Why did the author have the hydrophobia plague washed away soon after Old Yeller was killed?
- Do you think Papa had to leave the family for another cattle drive?
- Why did Travis laugh until he cried when he saw Little Arliss in the drinking water at the end of the novel?
- Did Burn Sanderson ever come back looking for Old Yeller?
- What did Travis do right after he shot Old Yeller?
- How did Mama learn about the methods of treating all the wounds?

Book Report Ideas

There are numerous ways to report on a book. After you have finished reading *Old Yeller*, choose one method of reporting on the book that interests you. It may be a way your teacher suggests, an idea of your own, or one of the ways that is mentioned below.

- **See What I Read?**

  This report is a visual one. A model of a scene from the story can be created, or a likeness of one or more of the characters from the story can be drawn or sculpted.

- **Time Capsule**

  This report provides people living at a future time with the reasons why *Old Yeller* is such an outstanding book, and gives these "future" people reasons why it should be read. Make a time capsule–type of design, and neatly print or write your reasons inside the capsule. You may wish to "bury" your capsule after you have shared it with your classmates. Perhaps one day someone will find it and read *Old Yeller* because of what you wrote!

- **Come To Life!**

  This report is one that lends itself to a group project. A size-appropriate group prepares a scene from the story for dramatization, acts it out, and relates the significance of the scene to the entire book. Costumes and props will add to the dramatization!

- **Into The Future**

  This report predicts what might happen if *Old Yeller* were to continue. It may take the form of the story in narrative or dramatic form, or a visual display.

- **Guess Who or What**

  This report is similar to "Twenty Questions." The reporter gives a series of clues about a character from the story in vague to precise, general to specific order. After all clues have been given, the identity of the mystery character must be deduced. (Use animal characters as well as human.) After the character has been guessed, the same reporter presents another "Twenty Clues" about an event in the story.

- **A Character Comes To Life!**

  Suppose one of the characters in *Old Yeller* came to life and walked into your home or classroom. This report gives a view of what this character sees, hears, and feels as he or she experiences the world in which you live.

- **Sales Talk**

  This report serves as an advertisement to "sell" *Old Yeller* to one or more specific groups. You decide on the group to target and the sales pitch you will use. Include some kind of graphics in your presentation.

- **Literary Interview**

  This report is done in pairs. One student will pretend to be a character in the story, steeped completely in the persona of his or her character. The other student will play the role of a television or radio interviewer, trying to provide the audience with insights into the character's personality and life. It is the responsibility of the partners to create meaningful questions and appropriate responses.

Research Activity

Directions: Here are some terms from *Old Yeller* that have to do with the farm, or were regional idioms (id.). Research the following and see how many you can find. Reference books that might be helpful are an unabridged dictionary, farm almanacs, tree and plant books, and books on American idioms. Your librarian might be able to help you.

Section 1
(Chapters 1-3)
cantle (n.)
fall to staves (id.)
tushes (n.)
javelina (n,; id.)
roan (adj.)

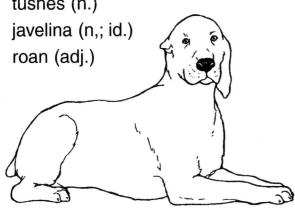

Section 2
(Chapters 4-6)
catclaw
scrub oak
windy (id.) (n.)
treed (v.)
hardpan (n.)
watercress (n.)
chaparral (n.)
sucking eggs
dog run
pack it

Section 3
(Chapters 7-9)
corncrib (n.)
boar coon
bee myrtle
in a strut (id.)
shoat (n.)
wall-eyed fit (id.)

Sections 4 and 5
(Chapters 10-16)
bear grass (n.)
chinaberry (n.)
turkey pear bush (n.)
corn shucks (n.)

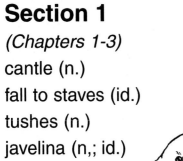

Changing the Ending

In this novel, Travis is forced to kill his beloved dog, Old Yeller, because the dog was bitten by the rabid wolf. The author, Fred Gipson, thought this was the appropriate way to end his story. However, there are other ways this novel could have ended.

Change the ending to *Old Yeller.* Perhaps you do not want the dog to be killed. Take another look at Chapters 15 and 16 to decide the best way to create a different ending. Be careful not to change the characters into something different from what the reader knows them to be. Write your new ending below.

_____

_____

_____

_____

_____

_____

_____

_____

_____

_____

_____

_____

_____

_____

_____

The Movie Version of *Old Yeller*

Since the Walt Disney film version of *Old Yeller* is readily available, many teachers will probably show it to their class. The following ideas are ways of making this a learning experience for your students. (It is suggested that you show the film after the reading. The visual element of film will often keep students from using their imaginations as they read if they view the film prior to reading. If some students have already seen the film, you do not have to worry about them giving away the ending to others. Travis "tells" the reader on the very first page that he must kill Old Yeller.)

- Have your students take a few notes during the film. You can give a general assignment such as asking students to find ten things different in the movie version. They can use these to make a Venn diagram of their own or you can do it as a group exercise for the entire class.

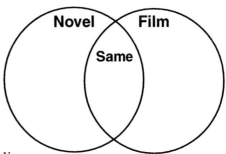

- Discuss how the screenwriter (one of the two was Fred Gipson) had to change the film in order to visualize Travis' thoughts. The novel is written in the first person; the film (as almost all are) is told from a third person's point of view.

- Discuss the actors in the film. Does Travis look as you expected? Is the actor's age about right? How about physical characteristics? Do the characters speak as you expected? Did you expect the Burn Sanderson character to be so tall? Was Mama prettier than you expected?

Have the students come up with some more questions comparing the actors in the film with the mental pictures students form of the characters in the novel.

More Comparisons

- How is the opening of the film different from the novel?

- How is Travis introduced to Old Yeller in the film?

- Is the 'Big Windy' Little Arliss tells different?

- How is the relationship between Bud Searcy and Lisbeth in the film different from the novel?

- How does the movie show Searcy's laziness?

- Why do you think the fight between the Roany and Chongo bulls was not filmed?

- What other large sections of the novel were not filmed?

- What was the heifer called in the movie?

- Do you think the movie moves too fast? (Example: Travis is hurt the first time he is marking the hogs in the film.)

- What is different about the way Old Yeller is treated after his fatal fight with the wolf in the film version? Which version do you prefer? Why?

Leads

A lead is how a story begins. Leads are the opening lines that draw a reader into the story. There are many different types of leads to try. Here are some that deal with the same situation. Observe how each one tells basically the same story in different ways.

Lead	Example
Typical or Description	Laura woke up early on Saturday. In two hours her club at school would be going on an all day trip to the local mountains. There would be time to play in the snow and slide down the hill on sleds. It was a day she had been looking forward to for weeks, but now it seemed ruined. Last night she and her best friend, Emily, had had a fight. They said some things to each other that could not be forgiven.
Action (a character doing something)	Laura opened her eyes and realized it was Saturday. She moaned loudly and buried her head in the pillow. The big day had come and it was going to be awful. How could she have fun playing in the snow after last night? She dragged herself out of bed and reached for her diary. She wrote furiously about her ex-friend, Emily, who had said some terrible things about her at the party last night. Should I go on the snow trip now?", she wrote in her diary. Absolutely, she thought. Why should that Emily keep her from going? She put on her warmest clothes for the snow trip, ate a quick breakfast of cereal and milk while talking to her mother, and ran to catch the bus.
Dialogue (a character or characters saying something)	"Emily has ruined my big day," Laura said to her mother as she came down for a quick breakfast. My ex-best friend has taken away the happiness I have been thinking about for weeks. I probably won't even play in the snow." Her mother said, "It can't be that bad. You will probably make-up with her on the bus." "No," Laura groaned. "This is the end of our friendship. I will never speak to her again as long as I live and if I meet her in heaven, I probably will ignore her there, too." "You're so dramatic," her mother laughed. "I bet you'll be talking to her before the bus gets to the mountains."
Reaction (a character thinking about something)	I better run or I won't make that bus. Mom could be so maddening sometimes. Speak to Emily? Never! Never! Never! That girl is off my list permanently and I am going to turn all my other friends against Emily, too. I'm going to show my mom how angry I really am. Even if Emily tries to speak to me, I will turn my back and walk away. I'll show Emily that she can't say those awful things to me and get away with it.

Leads *(cont.)*

Choose an event from *Old Yeller* and tell it in the four different leads discussed on page 40. Remember that the basic information is the same. The event is presented from different points of view.

Here are some possibilities:

✔ How Travis will handle the responsibilities of the farm when Papa is gone

✔ Travis' feelings about Yeller when the dog first comes to the Coates farm

✔ Travis deciding whether Old Yeller must be killed after being bit by the mad wolf

✔ Travis finally starting to be feel better at the end of the novel

On the lines below, write two different leads from a chosen topic. Read these to the class and ask them to determine which leads you used.

_____

_____

_____

_____

_____

_____

_____

_____

_____

_____

Now that you have tried the leads by re-telling a part of *Old Yeller*, you can try a story of your own. It can take place whenever you would like. Perhaps you would like to include an animal as one of the characters. It can be a wild animal or a pet like Old Yeller. Begin the story by trying two different leads.

Unit Test

Matching: Match the quotes with the description of the correct person or animal.

Travis   **Old Yeller**   **Bud Searcy**

Little Arliss   **Jumper**

Mr. Coates   **Bell**

1. _____ "his short hair was a dingy yellow..."

2. _____ "...how tall and straight and handsome he looked, with his high-crowned hat and his black mustache..."

3. _____ "I was fourteen years old, pretty near a grown man."

4. _____ "He was nearly as old as I was. We'd had him ever since I could remember. He'd protected me from rattlesnakes and bad hogs when I was little."

5. _____ "He'd scream when he was happy and scream when he was mad..."

6. _____ "...he was a red-faced man with a bulging middle who liked to visit around the settlement..."

7. _____ "...he was a dun mule with a narrow black stripe running along his backbone between his mane and tail."

True or False: Write true or false next to each statement below.

1. _____ Travis saw how valuable Old Yeller would be as soon as he found the dog.

2. _____ The bear fight made Travis realize how much he loved his little brother.

3. _____ Both Bud Searcy and Burn Sanderson warned Travis about the dangers of hydrophobia.

4. _____ Travis went directly home after the pigs slashed his leg.

5. _____ Travis knew that his mother was right when she said that Old Yeller had to be killed.

Sequence: Number these events in the order in which they occurred in the story.

_____ Old Yeller fought off the mad wolf.

_____ Old Yeller saved Travis from the killer hogs.

_____ Old Yeller saved Little Arliss from the she bear.

_____ Old Yeller stole the salt pork.

_____ Old Yeller refused to get involved in the bull fight.

Paragraphs: Answer the following in paragraph form on the back of this sheet.

1. Discuss how Travis carried out his responsibilities as the "man around the farm."

2. Discuss how Travis was able to get over the sadness of killing Old Yeller.

42

Response

Explain the meaning of each of these quotations from *Old Yeller*.

Chapter 1: "He made me so mad at first that I wanted to kill him. Then, later, when I had to kill him, it was like having to shoot some of my own folks."

Chapter 1: "He reached out his hand, and we shook. It was the first time I'd even shaken hands like a man. It made me feel me feel big and solemn and important in a way I'd never felt before."

Chapter 2: " 'And while you are gone, I want you to do some thinking on what I said about Little Arliss and this stray dog.' "

Chapter 3: "It didn't seem right and fair to me. How could I be the man of the family if nobody paid any attention to what I thought or said?"

Chapter 4: "When that happened, Chongo was suddenly the silliest looking bull you ever saw."

Chapter 5: "Well, Little Arliss was a screamer by nature."

Chapter 6: "So it was only natural for me to come to love that the dog that saved him."

Chapter 7: " 'Why, that old rogue!' she said. 'We'll have to figure some way to keep him from prowling Everyone in the settlement will be mad at us if we don't.' "

Chapter 8: "The man tied his rope around Old Yeller's neck and mounted his horse. That's when Little Arliss caught on to what was happening. He threw a wall-eyed fit."

Chapter 9: "But Papa had told me right from the start that fear was a right and natural feeling for anybody, and nothing to be ashamed of. 'It's a thing of your mind, he said, 'and you can train your mind to handle it just like you can train your arm to throw a rock.'"

Chapter 10: "But when I set out, it wasn't in the direction of home. It was back along the trail through the prickly pear."

Chapter 11: " 'Now, Arliss,' Mama said, 'you sit there on the pillows with Old Yeller and help hold him on. But remember now, don't play with him or get on top of him. We're playing like he's sick, and when your dog is sick, you have to be real careful with him.' "

Chapter 12: "I said, 'I guess Little Arliss will like it,' then knew I'd said the wrong thing."

Chapter 13: "Mama slammed the door shut, then turned to me. 'Spot made fight at me,' she said. 'I can't understand it. It was like I was some varmint that she'd never seen before.' "

Chapter 14: "He was still thin and rough looking and crippling pretty badly in one leg. But I figured he knew better than I did whether or not he was able to travel. I didn't call him back. As it turned out, it's a good thing I didn't."

Chapter 15: " 'But Mama,' I said. 'We don't know for certain. We could wait and see. We could tie him or shut him up in the corucrib or some place till we know for sure.' "

Chapter 16: " 'And a man can't afford to waste all the good parts, worrying about the bad parts. That makes it all bad... You understand ?' "

Teacher Note: Choose an appropriate number of quotes for your students.

Conversations

Work in size-appropriate groups to write and perform the conversations that might have occurred in each of the following situations.

- Travis asks his father if he can accompany him on the cattle drive. (2 people)

- Travis and Little Arliss talk about how they feel with their father away so long. (2 people)

- Travis tells his mother that he has thought it over but still thinks that the "thieving stray dog" has got to go. (2 people)

- Travis tells Mama how the bear fight made him realize how much Little Arliss meant to him. (2 people)

- Travis thanks Lisbeth for not telling anyone that Old Yeller was the dog that had been stealing from the settlement. (2 people)

- Mama and Little Arliss thank Burn Sanderson for letting the family keep Old Yeller. (3 people)

- Travis tells Burn Sanderson how he really feels about the danger of hydrophobia. (2 people)

- Travis thanks his mother for going to rescue Old Yeller and for taking care of the dog's wounds. (2 people)

- Travis tells Bud Searcy that he shouldn't expect his mother to cook for him and his granddaughter when she has so many other things to do. (2 people)

- Travis apologizes to Lisbeth for not appreciating the puppy she brought him. (2 people)

- Mama and Lisbeth discuss how to take care of Travis while he's healing from his leg injury. (2 people)

- Travis thanks Lisbeth for being such a big help to his mother while he and Old Yeller were gettingwell. (2 people)

- Travis tells Mama how he felt after he had shot Old Yeller. (2 people)

- Travis tells Papa about killing Old Yeller. (2 people)

Bibliography of Related Reading

Fiction—Stories about Dogs

Burnford, Shiela. *The Incredible Journey.* (Little, 1961)

Draper, Cena C. *The Worst Hound Around.* (Westminster, 1978)

Erickson, John R. *The Original Adventures of Hank the Cowdog* (Texas Monthly, 1988)

Estes, Eleanor. *Ginger Pye.* (Harcourt, 1972)

Gauch, Patricia L. *Kate Alone.* (Putnam, 1980)

Gipson, Fred. *Curly and the Wild Boar.* (Harper, 1979)

Little Arliss. (Harper, 1978)

Savage Sam. (Harper, 1962)

Farley, Walter. *The Great Dane Thor.* (Dell, 1980)

Griffiths, Helen. *Grip: A Dog Story.* (Holiday, 1978)

Hall, Lynn. *Halsey's Pride.* (Macmillan, 1982)

Kjelgaard, James A. *Big Red.* (Bantam, 1945)

Knight, Eric. *Lassie Come Home.* (Dell, 1940)

Koehler, Williarn. *A Dog Called Lucky Tide.* (Scholastic, 1988)

Little, Jean. *Different Dragons.* (Viking, 1987)

London Jack. *Call of the Wild.* (Macmillan, 1965)

White Fang. (Airmont, 1985)

Rawls, Wilson. *Where the Red Fern Grows.* (Bantam, 1974)

Shura, Mary Francis. *Mr. Wolf and Me.* (Scholastic, 1982)

Taylor, Theodore. *The Trouble with Tuck.* (Doubleday, 1989)

Terhune, Albert. *Lad: A Dog.* (Dutton, 1973)

Fiction—Other Animals

Adler, C. S. *Carly's Buck.* (Clarion, 1987)

Bagnold, Enid. *National Velvet. (Morrow, 1985)*

Campbell, Barbara. *A Girl Called Bob and a Horse Called Yoki.* (Dial, 1982)

Collura, Mary-Ellen Lang. *Winners.* (Dial, 1986)

Eckert, Allan W. *Incident at Hawk's Hill.* (Little, 1971)

Farley, Walter. *The Black Stallion.* (Random, 1977)

Fleming, Susan. *The Pig at 37 Pinecrest Drive.* (Westminster, 1981)

George, Jean Craighead. *Summer of the Falcon.* (Macmillan, 1979)

Graeber, Charlotte Towner. *Grey Cloud.* (Macmillan, 1979)

Gulley, Judie. *Rodeo Summer.* (Houghton, 1984)

Howard, Jean G. *Half a Cage.* (Tidal Press, 1978)

Kjelgaard, James A. *Haunt Fox.* (Bantam, 1981)

Manley, Seon. *A Present for Charles Dickens.* (Westminster, 1983)

Sewell, Anna. *Black Beauty.* (Airmont, 1974)

Shactman, Tom. *Wavebender: A Story of Daniel au Fond.* (Henry Holt, 1989)

Thomas, Joyce Carol. *The Golden Pasture.* (Scholastic, 1986)

Vail, Virginia. *Pets are for Keeps.* (Scholastic, 1986)

Westall, Robert. *Blitzcat.* (Scholastic, 1989)

Wilson, A. N. *Stray.* (Watts, 1989)

Nonfiction

Alter, Judith. *Growing Up in the Old West.* (Watts, 1989)

Benjamin, Carol L. *Dog Training for Kids.* (Howell, 1988)

Birch, Beverly. *Louis Pasteur.* (Stevens, 1990)

Cross, Helen R. *Life in Lincoln's America.* (Random House, 1964)

Freedman, Russell. *Children of the Wild West.* (Tickner, 1983)

Animal Superstars: *Biggest, Strongest, Fastest, Smartest.* (Prentice, 1984)

Hilton, Suzanne. *The Way It Was—1876.* (Westminster Press, 1975)

Laylock, George and Ellen. *How the Settlers Lived.* (David Mckay, 1980)

Phillips, Betty Lou and Bryce. *Texas.* (Waus, 1987)

Rainbow in the Sky: A Collection of Poetry, collected and edited by Louis Untermeyer. (Harcourt, Brace, 1963)

Silverstein, Alvin and Virginia B. *Dogs: All About Them* (Lothrop, 1986)

Smith, Jack. *Cats, Dogs, and Other Strangers at My Door.* (Watts, 1984)

Stein, R. Conrad. *The Story of the Lone Star Republic.* (Childrens, 1988)

Tunis, Edwin. *Frontier Living* (World, 1961)

Answer Key

Page 10

1. One reason was the "yeller" color and the other was the sound he made when barking.
2. The family lives in Texas, right after the Civil War (late 1860's).
3. Papa needs to earn more money for the family than his farm can produce.
4. Travis has to deal with the animals, take care of the corn patch, and watch after his mother and little brother.
5. Travis begins doing the chores without his mother asking him to.
6. Travis asks his father for a horse of his own.
7. Travis becomes angry at Yeller for eating the family's meat and at Mama for saying that he should let Arliss have Old Yeller.
8. Travis needs to kill a doe because the family needs meat to eat.
9. Travis hangs fresh cuts of venison where Yeller had stolen the other meat. He thinks if Yeller steals more meat, Mama will be forced to get rid of the dog.
10. Travis and Arliss fight like most brothers, but Travis, being older, is concerned with the safety of his little brother.

Page 15

1. Accept appropriate summaries.
2. Travis has a bullwhip in his hands and Yeller thinks Travis is going to hurt him.
3. When the Roany falls in the cart and goes rolling down the hill, the Chongo looks after him and can not understand what has happened.
4. Travis does not see the danger of the bulls fighting so near to their house. He and his family are too close to the fight and are almost killed by the charging bulls.
5. Little Arliss tries to catch and keep every living creature that he sees.
6. Travis and Mama were not able to get across the clearing to save Arliss before the mother bear could attack him. Old Yeller attacks the mother bear and saves the little boy.

7. Old Yeller is too small to actually hurt the mama bear, but the dog keeps the bear occupied so that the family can run for safety.
8. After the bear fight, Travis can not do enough for Old Yeller. The dog has saved his little brother and Travis cares for him very well after that.
9. Bud Searcy and his granddaughter, Lisbeth live in the area and would sometimes visit Travis and his family. Searcy usually has some news for the family, but really comes for a meal. The family does not like Searcy, but is fond of Lisbeth.
10. Lisbeth promises she will not tell that Yeller has been stealing eggs and food from the settlement. She will keep the secret because Yeller is the "papa" of the pups her dog, Prissy, will have.

Page 18

1. 577 miles, 929 kilometers
2. 278 miles, 447 kilometers
3. by way of Austin
4. 367 miles, 591 kilometers
5. Amarillo
6. Answers will vary.

Page 20

1. Accept appropriate summaries.
2. Travis keeps Old Yeller in the bedroom so he won't run around at night stealing food from the settlement.
3. Travis and Old Yeller sleep in the corn patch to keep the raccoons from eating the family's corn.
4. Ever since Old Yeller frightened Spot, all Yeller has to do is stand in front of the cow while she is being milked, and the cow will not move.
5. Burn Sanderson is looking for his dog.
6. Sanderson sees how much the family needs Old Yeller, and how much Little Arliss loves the dog.
7. Sanderson tells Travis that "there's a plague of hydrophobia making the rounds."

Answer Key *(cont.)*

8. Settlers brand their hogs with a special mark.

9. Travis climbs a tree and pulls one hog up at a time with his rope. He brands the hog and then lowers him down.

10. Yeller rounds up the wild hogs and leads them under the tree where Travis is sitting on a branch.

Page 25

1. Accept appropriate summaries.

2. Travis' father had told him about a bat cave and he hoped to see it.

3. Travis stands on a dirt bank. Unfortunately, the bank breaks and sends Travis falling in the middle of the angry hogs.

4. Travis is slashed in the calf of his right leg and the tusk goes all the way to the bone.

5. Travis has to make sure Yeller is safe before he leaves for home.

6. Travis says that he will not go to bed until they get Yeller.

7. Mama sends Little Arliss to look for a lizard in order to keep him out of the way while she sews Yeller's wound.

8. Yeller is placed on a piece of cowhide that Jumper pulls behind him.

9. Mama has to do all the work herself because Travis' is so bad all he can do is rest in bed.

10. Lisbeth brings Travis one of Prissy's pups. Travis hurts too much to be polite and just says that Little Arliss will probably like the pup.

Page 30

1. Accept appropriate summaries.

2. Lisbeth does almost everything Travis did, including bring water, feed chickens, pack in wood, cook, wash Arliss, and change Travis's bandage.

3. At first, Mama and Travis think Spot ate some pea vine.

4. Mama says they have to burn the bull's carcass because if animals eat it, they might spread the hydrophobia.

5. Travis is afraid some more of the cattle or even one of the family might get hydrophobia.

6. Travis feels that "it was going to kill something inside of me to do it, but I knew then that I had to shoot my big yeller dog."

7. Once Travis knows Old Yeller has to be killed, he does it quickly. He knows that Yeller might bite Arliss or someone else and then that person will die of hydrophobia.

8. Travis doesn't really care about the horse because all he can think about is killing Old Yeller.

9. Papa's advice to Travis about feeling better is "that a man can't afford to waste all the good part (of life) worrying about the bad parts. That makes it all bad."

10. Watching Little Arliss playing with the little pup and hearing Papa's laugh makes Travis begin to feel better.

Page 42

Matching

1. Old Yeller	5. Little Arliss
2. Mr. Coates	6. Bud Searcy
3. Travis	7. Jumper
4. Bell	

True or False

1. False	4. False
2. True	5. True
3. True	

Sequence

5 - 4 - 3 - 1 - 2

Paragraphs

1. Accept appropriate responses. Check that examples clearly support the writer's opinion.

2. Accept appropriate responses. Check to see that the writer uses examples that are from the novel.

Page 43

Accept all reasonable responses.

Page 44

Perform the conversations (dramas) in class. Ask students to respond to the conversations in several different ways, such as, "Are the conversations realistic?" or, "Are the words the characters say in keeping with their personalities?"

Answer Key *(cont.)*

48